Easy Self Hypnosis Techniques
Become the master of your own mind

Christophe Pank

Table des matières

Author of :

1/ My first steps on the Law of Attraction (Feb 2013)

2/ Journey of a Hypnosis practitioner against cancer (Fev 2015)

3/ Hypnosis and Pain Management : The study of the Hypno-Analgesia Process (Jul 2015)

4/ Limited Power : Accepting our own limits is to open up our real potential (May 2016)

5/Hypnosis and Hypnotic Gastric Band (Jan 2017)

6/ Hyperempiria and Self-Mastery : Apply Hyperempiria for your personal development (Jul 2017)

7/ Energetics CT (Sept 2017)

Introduction

While writing the previous book **« I could but I don't want to »,** I was continuing my practice and most of all my exchanges with my loved ones.

These loved ones, from work, my personal life, for some of them know about hypnosis.

However through seminars, outings with Street Hypnosis, in diverse exchanges, I realised that many didn't know really about Self-Hypnosis.

I imagine that many of you who read this book, do it because you want to use hypnosis in your every day life.

Self Hypnosis is the part of Hypnosis which will allow you to enter into an hypnotic state, a Trance, so that you can work on your subconscious. Do you know that for some practitioners, the Hypnotist do not bring his/her partner in Trance but teach him/her to activate his/her own Auto-Hypnosis.

Hypnosis is a state which is natural. You live trances many times a day :

- When you fix your interlocutor and that you go into your thoughts.
- When you have the name of your interlocutor burried into your mind...and no, nothing will do for you to remember it.
- When your feet hurt with your new shoes but that, during your evening party you didn't feel any hurt...until you go back home.

- When you are sure to have seen your phone in your bag...but it isn't.
- When you look for keys that were right in front of you from the beginning, but just appeared.

I think at least one of these examples would be a situation you lived already ? This is Hypnosis in your daily routine. This state of Trance allows you to connect with your subconscious. Your subconscious is this part of your spirit which guides your life most of the time, without you knowing.

It is also your best ally. In Trance, the dialogue between your Conscious and Subconscious is allowed. Hypnosis, at first, is somehow kind of like IKEA furniture.

We know it will look good once made at home, but when you open the box...you don't understand and it really seems like the notice is in chinese and not in english. If you are a handy person, there is nothing more simple to build. Hypnosis is just the same, we know it is going to make us feel better, we never find the right notice, and we tell ourselves that only « some » people can achieve it.

HnO Hypnosis, our practitioner group, try to simplify as much as possible how to learn methods such as Hypnosis and Auto-Hypnosis. We really want that the tool of Auto-Hypnosis can become a support, a habit, in your life.

This book will be like your HomeBase store, your D system of your Subconscious.

It permits to initiate bases of your internal union to provoke a real change in your everyday life. This learning process will ask you **regularity,** even the simplest things need to be mastered. I am sure that your desire to move on will give you great pleasure in your study and in the succes of the discovery of your infinite potential.

1/ What are you looking for ?

You have in your hands a book about Self-Hypnosis (SH). In Neuro-Linguistic Programming (NLP) we explain that all communication has a goal. Goals, even small ones, allow us to direct easily **our positive intention** towards a target.

You understand that without a target, there is no need in shooting an arrow and so, of practicing. You have within yourself **the most powerful computer ever,** not counting that it is an evolving system.

Your brain is capable of making you move on in all directions. Take a few minutes and write down simply three goals you would like to reach through Self-Hypnosis.

Are you looking to improve one of your capacities ?

Would you like to change one of your habits ?

Are you trying to change your perception on some specific things ?

For myself, the Self-Hypnosis, and the experience I had with them, makes me think that we really can become **the actors of our dreams.**

Write down your three goals here :

____

____

____

Well done !

Now, let's look at them and check that you have chosen them well. We can all decide to become billionaires but there are a few things to consider.

We are going to look at your three goals with the method SMART.

Check if each goal desired meets these criteria :

- **Specific :** Are you sure of its accuracy ?
- **Measurable :** When will you know that you succeed ?
- **Accessible :** where are you at today ? If you want to be a champion of 100 meters, you should really be practicing a lot.
- **Realistic :** Goals are steps for higher aspirations.
- **Temporal :** What are your deadlines ?

You are wondering why I didn't mention these points before ? Because of your Critical Factor.The Critical factor is your thoughts space which refrains every new information.

To go around it and erase this « resistance », you just need to offer an internal dialogue.

The most extraordinary tool for this is **the question**.

Now that you have taken the time to ask yourself these questions, are you satisfied of your goals and ready to go on ?

Start an adventure = Write Goals + Measure workability

2/ Discovery of a path

I am going to indicate to you what we are going to realise step by step in this book. We are going to create a path, **simple and quick,** so that you can unify yourself to your subconscious.

Schools and practitioners all have a different lexicon. I will give you definitions of the terms as we use them in HnO.

- **Conscious :** Analytical and Logical Spirit/ Short term memory. It is the Cogitum that we develop since childhood.
- **Subconscious :** Feelings and Emotions / Protector side/ Long term memory.
- **Unconscious :** Immune System and vital functions
- **Critical Factor Critique :** Security sas which validate or not coming informations between Conscious and Subconscious.

You are going to connect your Conscious and your Subconscious. Our education teaches us that our Will is the path to success. Paradoxically the will is rational and so part of the Conscious.

You probably read books about personal development.

Authors ask you to connect to your goals through emotions. The more you feel, visualise and vibrate, the more your subconscious is full of it.

Emotion is the perfect way to connect with your subconscious.

Here is a simple exercise :

- Take a deep breath.
- Remember an agreeable moment.
- Inhale while you play the scene in your imagination.
- Exhale slowly to project yourself in the scene.
- Take away all the details of the scene, colors, sensations, words, laughters, sounds, smells...
- Stay a bit into this emotion.
- Take a deep breath.

So easy, you feel good right ?

You can see that an emotion, negative or positive, can bring you to an hypnotic state. Anger is a form of **Active Trance**. Indeed, you can note that no logical comments come through to the furious interlocutor. He/she is closed in his/her emotion. We can notice that the Cogitum block the dialogue between **Conscious and Subconscious.**

It does it because you have taught it this since childhood. You need to **think of everything,** control everything, analyse everything.

Let's be honest, we are good and conditionned soldiers for the Society to be able to bring us into Trance and « pass on logically » messages. You can see it constantly on TV, political arguments and all form of teachings.

By the way, do you know that you always were in hypnotic state until your 6th birthday ?

This step can be explained with our other killjoy : **critical factor.** At HnO Hypnosis, we considere this critical factor as an airsas which keep informations. We are well made. Nature made us in a way that all new « informations » go through steps before their validation or integration in our subconscious.

It is a trial by fire for our new « beliefs ».

I am right now explaining to you a new concept, for most of you, it is a new discovery. Information go through our conscious which will try to sort it in your knowledge base and store it where other similar information are to match them up.

For those who have knowledge in Hypnosis, you are validating the information I give you. For those who have « similar practices », you modify the terms I am using so that it makes sense in your « world map ».

These two cases look like this :

→ From your conscious → through your critical factor → before the integration in your subconscious.

We can also have a group which have different knowledge of the same process, they will accept some aspect and leave some other for « reflexion ».

In this case, here is the path taken :

→ Your conscious → Your critical factor (Reflexion sas)

The information will be either rejected or accepted by your Subconscious. The last group rejects completely what I say and, in this case, their Conscious will list counter-arguments.

You can see that one concept will encounter a lot of blocage situations before being validated in the Subconscious. The information that we will want to integrate in Hypnosis is named : **suggestion**.

You understand now that we need a tool to accelerate its validation. This tool is called 'Trance' and you will master it very easily.

Here is a possible definition of Hypnosis :

It is a technique that allows to go around the Critical Factor and simplify the interaction between Conscious and Subconscious.

We are going to study what it does mean.

Informations + Conscious + Critical factor + Subconscious = Path of a Suggestion without Hypnosis

3/ Communication Conscious/Subconscious mind

You can easily understand that we want to find an efficient way to work on the programs we have registered within our Subconscious. While in Trance, we can build a **new internal scheme.**

We find back the belief that Hypnosis « sedate » participants of the experience. I then let you imagine how usefull it is to practice Auto Hypnosis if it is only to put yourself to sleep and then waken up a few minutes later.

The « hypnotic sleep » is in no way comparable to the nocturnal sleep. In facts, we are just going to « put to sleep » the Critical Factor. This action will cause an **agitation.** At HnO Hypnosis, we spend number of hours in the street, parcs to present ourselves, and eventually make available Hypnosis to people.

We are lucky to have many people who take the time to listen and try. The main feedback we received is that they stay awake and aware of what happen and most of all, that it is an agreeable experience.

Didn't it arrive that you drive for hours ? After a while, your Conscious gets use of the road and your Critical Factor disappear.

You do not pay any attention to the road anymore, you realise that your spirit was somewhere else or maybe a car suddenly comes right in front of you.

You have a reflex that make you react with the brake, the steer... It maybe happens that you told yourself how you « felt » that something was going to happen. In these moments, you are in an hyperconscious state, a form of Trance.

You will realise that most of the time, when we are too much in our thoughts, when we analyse events, words, situations, nothing seem easy. By the way, we use often the expression that « it gives us a headache ». We can't find the answers that will bring us peace. On the opposite, how many times were you so deep into your thoughts, in the train, underground, bus or walking, that you didn't realise the time.

Subconscious mind took back its place and everything seem « different ». Time seems shorter, we call this a **time distorsion.** Your perceptions are different as if everything was easier.

At these moments, you are in Trance.

Our Subconscious has been put **aside** in our life. We want the Conscious to control and direct the boat as a good captain. In this approach of life which has been **anchered**, we are at war with our Subconscious that wishes to express itself. It is very frequent that we **don't listen to it** at all, we become more and more rigide.

You must know people who want to control everything, handle everything. I am one of them.

I practice fighting sport since two decades. Martial arts put forward the « mind of steel ». More I was living this « restraint » of control, in my emotions, body, thoughts, and more I found that it was bringing an **imbalance**. I looked into the life expetancy of « Masters », in particular Japonese, who were known to have very strict and rigide schools.

I realise that most of them died young and in illnesses. The more schools were hard, the more they were loosing control and their life quickly. We are living in a society which function the same way.

We are orientated to **control** our emotions, desires, words, personality. We develop at its paroxism our **critical spirit.** It is not a surprise that, as controllers of our lives, we are **not able to handle** our fears, anxiety, stress and the one that the world imposes on us.

We disconnect from a part of ourselves : our Subconscious mind. Remember, in our Subconscious is found our emotions, preservation instinct.

I am not saying that the world is telling us to not preserve yourself... It seems that if we connect to the Matrix of the World, we forget the best teacher, friend, brother that we have...ourselves.

I am sure that you understand more and more that Auto-Hypnosis will permit you to find a **natural balance.** You will, finally, **allow the meeting, without any restraint,** your Yin and your Yang.

Today, we live a bit like in a world where we only communicate through Mails, SMS or phone calls. For our Conscious and our Subconscious it is the same. We will allow a real union, simple, authentic.

During sessions of Hetero Hypnosis, I observed that during a Trance state, the partner who lives the session astonished himself. He was stunned of everything he saw, felt and said during the session. I amused myself explaining that for once that the Subconscious is heard and allowed to speak, **he speaks loud.**

See that word « loud ». We are in a society that build stress. We « hold on » and we go towards different activities which allow us to « relax ».

These activities unite body and spirit. The Conscious and the Subconscious.

Direct dialogue + Relaxation = Hypnotic Communication

4/ The Critical Factor

We have to find the right network so that **our suggestion gets an answer.** Today you are kind the owner of a great cellphone in which you didn't put in the right SIM card to use. We quickly are going to discover what the Critical Factor proposes to us as alternative.

I know that presenting the Critical Factor as blocking, we can easily think that it is a disagreement. All in the nature brings good and less good. Yes, this security sas forbids us to be in Trance whenever we would like to (at the beginning), but it also **protects us.**

I go back to what I was explaining previously. As a child, we didn't have any Critical factor. If we teach to a child that Pepsi is water, all his/her life he/she will think so.

Imagine the number of **programs** than you have within yourself, that your parents, teachers injected and that today **do not fit you anymore.** You accepted what was expressed as true. You needed a dashboard of **« reference of beliefs ».**

Your « map of the world » is not really yours, more a part of your two initial teachers. Now that you are an adult, you put in place personal « beliefs ». Your Critical Factor is here to accept or refuse external elements.

To « insert » within you new database, what is proposed must recall one of your integrated « belief » in your Subconscious.

Otherwise, you have to repeat the new « information » enough so that the Critical Factor considere is as an **Habit**. A Habit becomes a known information and so becomes **uncriticable.**

My father always told me « the art of education is the art of repetition ». This man is an hypnotist. Take a few seconds to observe this phenomenon. I like to take the exemple of the trafic regulations. We all agree on the fact that it is a set of common rules for the well being of all. If we drive over white lines which are only lines on the floor and there is many.

However, with a lot of **repetitions** and manipulating fear, we succeed to get used of not going over them, **these notions are accepted** by the Subconscious. Now, if you go over a line or worse drive through a red light, don't you have **an emotion** of guilt ?

Even the more rogues of us, have a pic of adrenaline when then pass a red light at 2h in the morning in a desert town. Your Conscious knows that there is noone, that you do not risk anybody's life but still, an **emotion erupts.**

Whatever if it comes from fear of the infraction or of a possible accident. You are conditionned by a norm so clobbered down that you can't go against without activating a **resistance**. You probably already realised, we all have a **resistance towards change.**

This resistance is justified, we have to go look into the Subconscious to change a program which was already in place.

We have our Critical factor which is able to filter informations Conscious towards Subconscious, you can easily guess that he does the same Subconscious to Conscious. We activate an « anti-piracy system ». It is a bit like you have Pin code to enter, now that you are connected. You have then a form of protection very powerful which will protect some moments and stifle others.

To « brake » this system, there is what institutions, movements groups or sects do : **mental-reconditioning.** They use Trances states which by definition go around the **Critical Factor.** Sometimes it happens under pressure, fear, obligation, repetition. There are many ways which can be put in place so that you do not « think » anymore.

I will use what Mr Lelay, ex President General of TF1(TV French Channel Like Foxin US or BBC) expressed in a very exquisite way : « For TV advertisement to be perceived, the brain of the viewers have to be available. Our shows have for vocation to do so : entertain it, relax it and prepare it in between two messages. What we sell to Coca-Cola, is human brain availability. » (2004). You probably noticed the word « relax ». It echoes the relaxation we talked about previously.

You understood that our first action in Auto Hypnosis, before even to work on **our suggestions**, is to build the bridge which go around the Critical Factor.

Anti Piracy System + Filter = Critical Factor

5/ The first bridge

We are going to build a first bridge over your Critical factor. We name this « bridge » a **By Pass** in the Hypnosis world. It is very simple, it will just needed to be practiced regularly.

In the next **7 days**, I advise you to put in place this first bridge. Its goal is for you to get used to enter **easily and quickly** in a Trance. The first thing you need to do is to find a place that **relaxes** you.

It is important that **you take time for yourself.**

You will succeed **in very few time** to put yourself into Trance where you want to. For now **take pleasure** in your learning. If possible, during this week, stay **always at the same place to do your exercises.**

You are going to create a « cocoon » of Self-Hypnosis. It is also what we call a **spatial anchor.**

You know this sensation of feeling good when you come back in a place where you lived beautiful things.

You are going to live the same thing.

Now, take a moment **to breathe.**

Breathing is an essential part of relaxation.

You know Yoga, Practitioners think that the key of it is found in **the breath.**

You are going to breathe 7 times, only with your nose and repeating internally to yourself : « I relax more and more. ». We are going to put in place the first bridge with a **Saturation of Senses.**

The Saturation functions on the simple fact that we can only do 5 (+/- 2) things at the same time, after we saturate. You already noticed what you feel in these cases, you can't think nor analyse.

It is a perfect moment to use a Trance.

1. Lift your head up at around 20°
2. Keep your eyes open
3. Keep your focus on a fixed point.
4. Breathe deeply during the whole exercise, try to breathe with your abdomen.
5. While continuing the previous point, pay attention to all sounds you hear.
6. Add to this the sensations you have in your feet and going up in your body.
7. While you go back up slowly, you always keep your attention to this fixed point and you let your vision includes more and more elements.
8. When you arrive to the head, you must have in your vision, the whole room you are in and hear each vibration.
9. When you feel this unity, to the next exhalation close your eyes.
10. Take as much time you want while repeating yourself : « More and more relaxed »

You just lived a Trance state put in place voluntarily.

You observed that the fact of taking all these elements at once **saturated you.** At this moment you ask yourself if you were really under Hypnosis. This is a natural question. As the state you just lived. I specified from the beginning that you live Hypnotic States daily.

Answer these questions :

- Do you feel more relaxed ?
- Do you feel more open and focused on things ?
- Is your breath deeper ?
- Do you feel a bit in the clouds ?

Welcome in YOUR Trance.

At HnO Hypnosis, we observed that according circumstances, subjects were going more or less deep in Hypnosis. Do this exercise a few times a day and take note of the similar times in the day when you are in a similar state.

Note them here :

____

____

Saturations + Relaxation + Repetitions = Mastery of the First Bridge

6/ The depth

We all are different and even if we can find ourselves in some similar states, some will naturally direct themselves towards **Deeper Trances.** We noticed that pesonal lives of each and every one will more or less develop possibilities « to go » in Trances.

A child who lived with violence, or to be clearer, in **a perception** of violence, within the family will have developped qualities of dissociation very close to Hypnosis. Take pleasure in always going deeper towards **a Relaxed Auto Hypnosis.**

You will observe that you will go further within yourself and that you will get out more relaxed. We are going to describe what represents a deepening. Before all, there is no good or bad in this notion. There are days, situations and moments in which we are going more or less deep.

I present to you the classification of the National Guild Of Hypnotists (NGH). This organisation is the biggest of the world, it gathers more than 15 000 hypnotists.

To every level of trance is linked an **Hypnotical Phenomenon** which allow to see the depth of the Partner's Trance. An Hypnotical Phenomenon is a reaction from the body and spirit to the suggestion.

The scale of the NGH is composed of 6 levels (Examples of the introduction page) :

1. Minor Catalepsy
1. Major Catalepsy
2. Amnesia
3. Anaesthesia
4. Positive Hallucination
5. Negative Hallucination

In Auto Hypnosis you will observe that you will not live any Hypnotical Phenomenon. However, **you will automaticaly** go to one of these levels.

It doesn't matter particularly that you go in a lower level at first. With the experience you will be able one day, if you decide to, to go to see the dentist without anaesthesia, you will have to be sure to be able to go to level 4. It is just like an habit, it will come in time.

So today, in your opinion, what level are you at ?

Trances + Levels = Deepenings

7/ Second Bridge

You worked on the **first bridge** for a little while. You are able to go back in Hypnosis just by looking at this text and by focusing on your breath....right ?

For now, we just studied one way to go into Trance. We are going to continue with simple techniques for you to go in Trance even more easily. This second bridge is based on Dave Elman's technique. I find it quite stunning. In the only book Dave Elman wrote « Hypnotherapy », he explains that the 6 years old girl of one of his student was using this method with success.

There is a verb in English : **To Pretend**.

You are simply going **to pretend** to be 6 years old and that you were playing a game. Are you ok to play ?

I told you that Hypnosis was **child play.** You are just going to close your eyes and relax your eyelids, then relax all muscles around your eyes. Then you imagine that you put three layers of magical glue on your eyelids.

Don't forget, you are 6 years old and you play.

A **first time,** just to relax even more your eyes.

A **second time,** just to be sure that you can't open your eyes.

A **third time,** to give you enough time to not want to open your eyes.

Now, try that you can't open your eyes. Like a child, observe that you can't.

Its is simple, right ?

The fact is that you can't open your eyes, simply because you don't want to and that, even though you try, you can't, you created a bridge between your Subconscious. You understand that the Critical Factor, which accept the fact that you can't open your eyes, opens simply the sas, without critic.

You can compare the two states you obtain with the first and the second bridge. We now just have to deepen the state within, you know how to connect yourself to quickly.

Act like you are a 6 years old child + Pretend = Second Bridge

8/ Deepeners

You succeed to enter into an Hypnose state. You used one of the two bridges presented. It is interesting to, according to the goals you have set up first, go through a **deepening step.** I am going to present you two methods extremely simple, very easily understandable.

The Fractionation

This method uses the principle well known of scuba diving. To go into the marinal depths, you need to go by steps. You are going to do the same with your trance.

Each time that you come back up from your Trance state, you only go back **further, deeper.** To do so you simply have to **open your eyes and close them** imagining that you double your relaxation state each time.

The first times, when you open your eyes, you will slightly get out of your trance. If **you sugest to yourself** that you are going back and deeper, your Subconscious will answer to your « order ».

The Splitting is very easy to put in place. It is composed as followed :

- Each time you open your eyes you inhale.
- A little break while your eyes are open.
- Close your eyes when you exhale.

Take a time to test right now, starting the bridge n°2. You can see or feel, that the more you practice, the more you are struggling to keep your eyes open.

Physiologicoly, **your body relaxes.** At first, do it ten times, taking your time and imagining each time that you **relax twice more.**

With the experience, you will only do it 3 times and get the same result.

The Countdown

The second technique to deepen your trance is **the countdown.** Today still I am astonished by the impact of this method which is so simple.

You just need to countdown 20 to 1 thinking that you are descending or climbing a staircase. In between number, take the time to **breathe deeply.**

You observe that your body, from itself, will relieve itself of a weight and enter into a real true relaxation of your muscles. More than just believing me, try it.

Do the n°2 Bridge then right after a Splitting followed by a Countdown and stay for a few minutes within the suggestion that you feel good. We are not going to see other deepening techniques. These two will allow you to easily reach the level 4. If you want to **go further,** it is very easy. For the Splitting you do it 30 times, for the countdown you start at 100.

In my opinion, **the level 4 of depth is excellent,** because you avoid going through the sleep and allows your Conscious to orientate its work with the Subconscious.

Relaxation + Respiration + Fractionation

+ Countdown = Deepenings

9/ The Suggestion

For some, Hypnosis is **an art of the suggestion.** It is true that the state you discovered **opens yourself.** This state **multiplies the impact** an idea in your Subconscious. There will be no critical barrier which will come and block the information.

The Suggestion is indeed **your best friend** when it comes to Trance. This is why during your week of Bridge n°1, I asked that you observe when you live this state in your daily life (Technique : Internal Focus).

You realised that, many times a day, you « go » into Trance. It is a great moment to repeat yourself **a positive suggestion.**

How can you build a suggestion ?

I like to take the concepts of mantras in personal development.

Your suggestion needs to be :

- Simple Sentence
- Short Sentence
- Positive Sentence
- Precise Sentence
- Progressive Sentence

Of all suggestions I read about, the sentence of Emile Coué stay an exemple.

« Every day from all points of view, I feel better and better ».

The only thing this affirmation doesn't take into consideration is precision. It stays very general. For your beginning, in your suggestions, you can **take this structure** adding just your goal.

For example :

« Every day from all points of view, I feel more and more relaxed ».

During your sessions in Auto Hypnosis, it is interesting to **fix yourself on a sentence.** During your Trance, you **multiply effects** of ideas and informations that you program in your subconscious.

The difference with the notion of positive thinking, which is oftenly to repeat twenty times the same thing, is found in the **Hypnotic State.** When you tell yourself 20 times : « I am fine, I am relaxed » and that you do it in your **normal mental attitute,** you go through your Critical Factor.

However, when you place yourself in a moment where your Critical Factor is « out », the information connects and **installs itself more and more** in your brain. Now that your goals are clearly defined in your head, put them into Positive Suggestions.

You now know the Process to insert a suggestion within your Subconscious. Before practicing, do not forget that Auto Hypnosis needs to have a **personal goal.** This is extremely important as many practice Auto-Hypnosis or Hypnosis to change others.

In life, it is not the external world that we need to change. **Change happens within us.**

Let's go back to our practice :

- Choose the bridge you want to use.
- Deepen to feel good.
- Take the time to breathe deeply.
- Repeat your suggestion.
- Build a mental image of your suggestion in your life.
- Develop emotions linked to your realised Goal.

Once you spent enough time you think is needed, get out of your Trance.

Positive Goals defined + Trance State = Impacting

10/ Mental Imagery

In the trainings I attended, Americans love to work around what they call the **Mental Imagery.** They are doing whole sessions about : how to build an Image so it take form into your spirit, that connect with your goals and which **realise yourself.**

There is a difference to make **bewteen imagine and image.** Some people, who aren't « visual » express some difficulties to imagine. As they don't see (visualise), they are then sure that they can't practice hypnosis or personal development work.

It is good to make the difference between the two terms. Whoever you are, **do you have the image** of a martian ? A surfing dwarf bear ? A martian hypnotising a bear while surfing ? There is very little chance that you already « saw » these scenes. If it is the case...you have a strong potential of Suggestions.

You can then, **without any difficulty,** have an image of your goal.

Is it a scene ? A sensation ? A sound ? An emotion ?

The form of your **image goal** doesn't matter, you will realise that you have it in you. Take the time to imagine or image your three Goals.

Amplify the different factors or details more and more for you.

Very good. You more and more give life to your goals. They become clearer and clearer. One of my teacher, Lee Pascoe, explains very well some details about the mental image. She says that an image that doesn't evolve will loose its impact on the Subconscious mind. She advises to make your image « alive ». With a dynamique, color, sensation taste.

Try it out :

- ⋏ Choose a Bridge
- ⋏ Deepen
- ⋏ Put in place your Suggestion
- ⋏ Repeat your Suggestion
- ⋏ Image it
- ⋏ Make it alive, evolving more and more

When you will feel good and connected to the success of your goal, come back to the here and now.

You will observe that more and more **this suggestion is integrated** to yourself. Though you only have spent a few instants to imagine it, to make it alive.

Image + Make the image alive = Mental Imagery

11/ The Length

Time is a **very relative** factor in the world of Hypnosis. There is no minimum needed to have surprising results. I am going to use one of the principles of **José Silva**, the founder of the Method Silva, who was a great Hypnotist.

He used to say that if you go in Trance for your goals once a day it is **good,** twice a day **very good,** three times a day **excellent.**

In the same way if you stay five minutes it is good, ten minutes very good, fifteen minutes excellent. The important thing is to do and **put in practice regularly** what you learn in this book or elsewhere.

The Self Hypnosis is **particularly accessible** and you must have realised that by now. The only necessary thing, is the **regular practice.** On my side, I worked on very various timings. At first, I was doing five minutes. Then, I developped my capacities more and more and I hold Auto Hypnosis sessions for more than an hour.

The regular practice showed me that very long timings are not constructive. Very often we don't succeed to keep the communication between the Conscious and Subconscious for a long period of time.

We are falling asleep or we are not active anymore in the process.

In this notion of not being active anymore, there is nothing negative. If you take the principle of the **unique suggestion**, you can give all freedom to your Subconscious.

At first, it is best to orientate the process.

It is a bit like a footing. If you didn't run since a long time you **pay attention to your breath.** With the experience you will not anymore, it will be automatic.

Let's take our time to **master the basis,** so that we can put in place our personal way to grow in it.

I come back more and more on a serie of suggestions I work for 5 minutes. With a timer to start the beginning and the end of the session.

You can put in place many suggestions by goals.

Find three suggestions by goal.

Goal 1 :

____

Suggestion 1 :

____

Suggestion 2 :

____

Suggestion 3 :

____

<u>Goal 2 :</u>

____

Suggestion 1 :

____

Suggestion 2 :

____

Suggestion 3 :

____

<u>Goal 3 :</u>

____

Suggestion 1 :

____

Suggestion 2 :

____

Suggestion 3 :

____

Perfect ! You have now **an ideal schedule** for your Auto Hypnosis.

Week

Morning	Time	Afternoon	Time	Evening	Time
Goal 1/ Suggestion 1	5 Minutes	Goal 2/ Suggestion 1	5 Minutes	Goal 3/ Suggestion 1	5 Minu
Goal 1/ Suggestion 2	5 Minutes	Goal 2/ Suggestion 2	5 Minutes	Goal 3/ Suggestion 2	5 Minu
Goal 1/ Suggestion 3	5 Minutes	Goal 2/ Suggestion 3	5 Minutes	Goal 3/ Suggestion 3	5 Minu

You only need to take 45 minutes a day, to relax yourself and to reach your goals.

Clear Suggestions + Defined Goals = Optimum Timing of Session

12/ Third Bridge

You now know how to enter in Trance with a few different techniques. Deepenings can be made **as you wish.** Suggestions are more and more clear. To stay in the study of an unique suggestion, there is a **method a little bit more advanced.**

This method was put in place byt the Hypnotist Jerry Kein. This is **simple.** The only thing you need to master to use it, is your **entry in Self-Hypnosis** almost instantly.

If you have a few repetitions to feel more comfortable, do it.

This technique can be presented as followed :

- Take a cardboard of the size of a **professional card**.
- Write on it your **suggestion.**
- Stretch your arm placing the card **between your thumb and index in front of your eyes.**
- **Read** ten times the sentence written.
- Your other hand is on your leg, the **index up** just like you were about to press a button.
- Fix the card to clearly see what is written on it and everything around (**Peripheral Vision**)
- Once ready to enter into your Trance, put your index down as you **activate** your Hypnotic State.
- Close your eyes and deepen, thinking only about your suggestion.

This practice is extremely **freeing.** You count on the perfect trust in your subconscious to anchor this suggestion. As I mentioned earlier, this method is interesting as soon as you feel comfortable to « handle » a session putting in place a **dialogue between your Conscious and your Subconscious Mind.**

We are in another form of Auto Hypnosis, in which the Subconscious take back all its place, it becomes a **monologue.** The Conscious is then very simply in the **reception** and not the issuance. I would advise to realise this Bridge, it is an excellent exercise which allows you to be conscious and to **trust your capacities.**

So that you can really let go, you are going to fix your attention to **your breathing.** Each time that you repeat the sentence by re-reading it, do it on **an Exhalation.**

In the same way, when comes the time « to close the light », do it on a long exhalation and let yourself be transported by your Subconscious. With the mastery of starting an Hypnotic State, this Bridge can become the simpler and the most efficient of all.

Take some time to repeat and perfect your two previous bridges. You can use the previous board and prepare your nine professional cards.

**Mastery of Trances + Work on Breathing +
Professional Cards = Third Bridge**

13/ Confort Zone

We practice Auto Hypnosis **in order to learn to handle** events from our daily life. Many practitioners want to **become calmer** and more relaxed. Maybe you have a deadline like an exam, an appointment, a match or stressful lives which don't allow rest.

You know that with this centennial method you are going to be able to work with the most extraordinary forces of the world. Your Subconscious is your guide and companion to **find back serenity.**

Here is a method that is very often used in disciplines like Sophrology, Yoga Nidra, etc... This time you are not going to work with suggested goals.

Next week you are going **to learn to let go.**

It is now two or three weeks, depending on how you progressed, that you have been working on Auto Hypnosis. For the next 7 days, **you are going to relax** your spirit which have been your excellent companion during your learning.

Choose one of the two bridge to go into Trance.

Once you are relaxed at a satisfying level, **imagine a corridor.** Once in this corridor, countdown 10 to 1 imagining a very bright door towards which you are walking to.

At one, you are going to **go through this door** to find yourself in a place you are going to build. This place needs to be appeasing that you know it in real or not.

It is actually better that **it doesn't bear any memories** of your life. This zone is yours and noone from your life has a space into it. You are going to take a moment to visit. Make sure you find some nature, a place to have some shelter. Let your **connection Conscious/Subconscious mind** bring you the keys.

This comfort place is where you are going to go to a few times per day in order **to relax youself, to let go.** The more you will build this place peaceful and agreeable, the more you will take pleasure in going back to it.

This creation **of your positive internal life** is the first interaction Conscious/Subconscious that you live. This principle of inventing mental image, in the hypnotic world, is going to be on of the lever of your evolution in your world of the Auto Hypnosis in the next weeks.

Build **a fully lively world.** You can hear the sounds of the waves from the ocean, feel the wind on your face, go to a warm source, a world where you feel good and that you can enjoy. The more you add consciously elements and the more you **will be astonished** to see that when you go back, this zone will have evolved.

It is not because your Conscious mind don't think of it, that your Subconscious doesn't do its job.

This zone is going to be **your appeasement,** and your trance will only be more agreeable. The more you go down and the more you will develop a sensation of feeling good.

It is a bit like taking care of a garden. You are going to enjoy seeing what you sow growing. You are going to enjoy taking care of this part of you.

This positive zone is completely yours.

Positives Images + Trances + Pleasure + Appeasements = Your Comfort Zone

14/ The tree of serenity

You probably put in place your comfort zone, which, as time goes by, becomes **more and more agreeable.** To continue this **dynamic of relaxation,** there is an exercise that will allow you to completely relax your body and thoughts.

You just need to go to your comfort zone, then, in a chosen place, to identify a big **strong and powerful tree.** Once you have imagine this tree, you are going to **project yourself in it.**

You are going to work a trance in connection with your body. It is a symbolic work, the tree represents the time of the session.

- Imagine gradually that your legs, feet are becoming the roots of the tree.
- That your body becomes the trunk.
- Your arms and hands are now the branches.
- Your head is the top.

You unite within you earth and sky. Now concentrate on your breathing. At each **deep inhaling,** imagine that **the energy of the earth** goes up all the way up of the tree. Just like if it nourishes it.

Once the inhaling is done, **retain** a few instants your breath and, doing so, leave the strenght regenerates you.

During the exhaling, imagine that the light of the sun comes on the tree, top to roots, sending all stress, tensions, deeply in the earth. Imagine during the session that your arms, your hands are light, as branches that sway into the wind.

Do this exercice during a few minutes.

Do not hesitate to let go of all blocking emotions that you lived today or in the week.

The most important being that you are in **the link Body-Conscious-Subconscious Mind.**

This method of Auto Hypnosis is an introduction **to live trances more active.** It is important that in the next weeks, you can utilise what you have been taught in all situations.

In your daily life, we are not closed in a peaceful room with time available only for ourselves. We are in a world that move, we have a work, friends, family...

Tools of Hypnosis can be used **whenever.**

This interaction with the tree will allow you to enjoy fully the links in your unity.

Controled Breathing + Conscious orientates images + Trance = Technique of the tree.

15 / The Tester

You start to realise that Auto Hypnosis can be made in an active dynamic. Remember, everyday and many times a day you have natural Trances starting whenever. We are going now to talk about a fun and useful notion.

The Tester, in Hypnosis is also called the Signaling.

It is a reflex from **the body** that you are going to put in place to dialogue with your Subconscious with the Yes or the No.

To do so, here is the initial process, now that you have experience :

- ⋏ Choose a Bridge.
- ⋏ Deepen.
- ⋏ Suggest your desire **to create a Pact** between Conscious/Subconscious.
- ⋏ Suggest that your **right Index** will move to say yes and your **left Index** to say no.
- ⋏ Connect your body to this dialogue repeating the following suggestion « **As soon as it is 'Yes' put up the right index (doing the movement), as soon as it is 'No' put up the left one (doing the movement)** ».
- ⋏ Ask simple questions like your first name/last name/If you wear this or that.
- ⋏ Once you are satisfied with the answer, get out of your Trance.

To continue this reflex, that you write within yourself, continue to ask yourself very simple questions all day long. You will observe the quality of the connection, even in the **awake state.**

The tester will allow you to not always go into Trance to have the answers to your questions.

You can use it for the choice of a meal in a restaurant, to know if the light is going to stay green or red... Do **very simple tests,** for you to get use to **trust** your subconscious.

At first, you are going to have wrong answers. It is normal, we also are in the rational and oftenly in the desire of an answer which fits us. To put in place a Tester consists in trusting the Subconscious, even if the answer doesn't fit what we want.

I know what it costs sometimes. It happened I didn't want to listen to the answer, though repetitive on the same question, hoping that my conscious desire will take the place of the information of my subconscious. I advise that you **use** this tester the more often possible in your daily life and to **regularly do your process** during 7 days.

Repeat this process regularly to **anchor it** deeper and deeper and you will obtain satisfying results quickly.

Once you feel that you master the tester, I would advise that you test your goals and suggestions. Take a moment for this and fill in the board asking yourself: « Is this goal really good for me ? »

If 'Yes' test each Suggestion, If 'No' it may be interesting to look back at your Goals :

Test	Yes	No	Test 2	Yes	No	Test 3	Yes	No
Goal 1			Goal 2			Goal 3		
Suggestion 1			Suggestio n 1			Suggestio n 1		
Suggestion 2			Suggestio n 2			Suggestio n 2		
Suggestion 3			Suggestio n 3			Suggestio n 3		

The more you use your Tester the more you will be able to be precise on what is good for you.

Ideomotor response + Link with Subconscious = Tester

16 / Another Aspect of Hypnosis

The more you progress in the study and the practice of the Auto Hypnosis, the more you will be able to **go further** in your experiences.

Let's summarise what we have seen so far.

- ⋏ The three Bridges that allow you to go in Hypnosis
- ⋏ Two Deepenings
- ⋏ The Comfort Zone for you to create a decompressing place.
- ⋏ The tree to empty your emotions and obstacles.
- ⋏ The Tester for you to know the answer Yes or No of your Subconscious.

You now have all **bases** to work on relaxing Trances, Goals which you have chosen. We are going to enter into another aspect of the Hypnosis with the following exercises. I always give to my Clients/Patients the possibility to **go back in Self Hypnosis,** with different exercices according to their issues.

Most of the time, they stay in their **Comfort Zone** to work.

Some of them comes with pains that can't be explained medically or chronic pains, we work in this case on an anchor of **well being state.**

They can then, almost instantly, **eliminate the pain** from their body, via a quick Trance. Others prepare deadlines, in sport, personal life or professional. Their Trance will, in this case, axe itself towards results of their body or spirit at a particular moment.

Self Hypnosis is allowing them to prepare an event the more **peacefully** possible. They know that at the right time, they will just have to **activate the program** they repeated under Hypnosis.

The emotional links and the lack of communication, in interpersonal realtionships can be diminished by what we name Subjective Communication. This type of communication permits us to free ourselves during a Trance of all we keep inside and not essential, even disagreeable. Keep in mind that Self Hypnosis is a tool **useful in your daily life.** It brings you positive answers to your regular difficulties.

The theme I am going to present here, can free you from stress and physical pain or emotional ones.

Analgesia + Motivation + Cut the Links = Advanced Self Hypnosis

17 / Pain Management

Our body is subjected to many attacks and agressions. It is frequent that we have pains. These can be joints, structurals but also migraines, abdominal pain …

We got use to the **Allophatic answer** and take medicine.

This habit was put in us before our Critical Factor works. You can see that for some it is an **immediate reflex** to go and take a product at the first sign of pain.

Pain is **Communication mode** that our body/Subconscious uses to present us a dysfunction.

It is a **messenger** that we quickly want to put out of action, without however **understand the message.** Hypnosis is used from its begnnings in pain management.

More and more we can find anaesthesists who work on **Hypno Anaesthesia.** Surgeries sometimes complex can be done under Trance.

As you study Hypnosis, you are perfectly capable of it. Without going to the anaesthesia, you are capable of **managing your pains.** Practicing sports, I had more or less important pains. I am not someone who like medicine (educative suggestion from my mother). I had then got used of **controling my pain.** At first I was doing it mentaly imposing myself to reduce my pain.

I had satisfying results though I was having long moments with a high level of pain, I simply learned to go over it.

It is the masochistic formula, which loses its interest when you know about Self Hypnosis. Now, I can go to the dentist without anaesthesia or going out of a surgery without developing pain.

It is not magical, if I can do it **you can do even more.** Before starting, you need to Master basics. If I ask you to put yourself into Trance immediately, you need to be able to do it. We are going to put into place a classic of Hypnosis. **The Analgesic Glove.**

To do so, you have to connect again to your body.

You are going to learn to listen to **sensations and changes** that you put yourself into place.

Take your **non dominant hand,** meaning the right one if you are left-handed and oppositely.

First step :

- Sit down and let your arm along your body.
- Do the bridge you like.
- Deepen.
- Be aware of your non dominant hand.
- Imagine that you put it into a freezing water basin.
- Let your Subconscious changing the sensation in your hand.
- Take a few minutes, you are going to be aware of the changes weither it is cold, tingling, light or weight sensation...
- Open simply your eyes.

You now know that you are capable of **transforming a perception.** This new perception, we are going to compare it to your other hand. Take a moment and observe at least 2 different elements.

Very good, go to the second step.

Second step :

- Close your eyes.
- Do a bridge.
- Deepen.
- Find the « different » sensations the quickest possible.
- Make it move into your arm, just as it was now freezing aswell.
- Open your eyes.

You start step by step to **coordonate your sensation to your suggestions.** The suggestion, in this case, is to transfer the sensation in another part of the arm.

Let's carry on.

Third step :

- ⚔ Close your eyes.
- ⚔ Deepen.
- ⚔ Reactivate your sensation.
- ⚔ Put this hand up and imagine that it is attracted to the top of your head.
- ⚔ Take a few minutes to do it.
- ⚔ Once your hand is over your head, keep it there.
- ⚔ Imagine that this sensation gets stronger and stronger.
- ⚔ When it is done, let your hand touch slowly your head.
- ⚔ Transfer this sensation of « appeasing cold » to your head.
- ⚔ Imagine that you apply a calming balm that goes down your body.
- ⚔ When you feel that the sensation of your body has been modified, open your eyes.

You just transformed **a suggestion into a physical sensation.** If you have a discomfort or pain, try it. You simply focus at first on this discomfort or pain.

- ⚔ Do a bridge.
- ⚔ Deepen.
- ⚔ Activate your hand.
- ⚔ Amplify your sensation of Appeasing Cold.
- ⚔ Let your hand go towards your discomfort.
- ⚔ Breathe deeply.
- ⚔ At each exhalation, imagine that you diffuse this sensation into your discomfort.
- ⚔ Once the discomfort is lessened or removed, open your eyes.

At first we use a lot the hand, with the experience **you will be able to simply orientate the appeasing sensation** by thinking of it, just like you did in transferring it from your hand to your arm. This method is **easy to assimilate,** the most important is to trust the suggestion and the sensations you build.

Your brain will answer to your order. The more you practice, the more you will realise that **you can manage your pain.**

However, it is crucial to understand that some of your pains are like signals which indicate you to go and **see a doctor or a medical specialist.**

Stay aware. It will happen naturally as you understood that you are able to be in contact with your body.

Appeasing Cold + Suggestion + Transfer = Pain Management

18 / Prepare yourself with the Self Hypnosis

Our society of performance is linked to a constraint of **permanent results.** We become more and more **machines** that have to « succeed » in all areas of their life. Effects can be perverse. Fear, stress, lack of confidence and self esteem appears in all areas.

You understand **better and better** how your Subconscious works and what it is able to bring you. However it is time to unplug your beliefs of what this world has « imposed » on you. Cut the chains of a behaviour which doesn't respond necessarily to who you are, but to what the world expects from you.

You feel more and more obliged and your stress and need of performance increase. It is possible that we are so much into our habits that we do not relativise anymore at all. It is usefull to see and perceive things on **different angles.**

You prepare at best, mentaly and physically, while not paying so much attention on feedbacks. You learn gradually that the way will be built with the feedback on different experiences, which will maybe make you go beyond your own goals.

I like one of the principle of NPL which is that **nothing is a failure.** All is a feedback to take into consideration for improvement.

We know, as much in sport that professionaly, that we can succeed **by optimising our body and spirit.** I was involved in many competition and I am not at all a fan of physical conditionning, I succeed to win titles with my mental preparation.

I was going « against » the worldwide and specifically « competitors » who absolutely wanted to win. I was thinking more as « Whatever if you don't win, the most important is that you don't loose ».

I enter a competition **focusing on not losing.**

It goes against the elements I expressed for the definition of a goal.

The notion to be position is not crucial. The most important is **the emotion in the statement.**

The mental is part of the athletes preparation. Let's take the example of one of my friend in Mix Martial Arts, **Johnny Frachey.** He is a professional fighter and he is followed by an excellent mental preparer. I was lucky to work with him aswell. It is an athlete extremely intelligent and well prepared. For him the fight is 80% happening in mental. Having been in the changing room with him before a fight, I observed that he put himself into trance before each fight.

All his preparation, before going into the ring, is to reactivate anchors, through music, Keys Sentences. In the same way you are able to prepare yourself with **everything you learned until now.**

Sportive Preparation before deadline

You have deadlines. You are going to work your **Trances during trainings.** You have moments where **you are satisfied of your game.** Maybe a technique or a training fight. As you learnt previously, Hypnosis is an active mode. You **can memorise good moments.** Your body put himself in the condition mental orientates it.

If you « memorised » positive instants, you will be **able to activate them whenever you want.** Each time that you are satisfied of what you put in place, put yourself in Auto Hypnosis and make **a move** like close your fist very strongly. You are going to assimilate this move to **the trust and success state.**

Sport puts one in Trance in general, optimise this internal moment to multiply it at its maximum. Each moment os success during training = Fist closed just as you take the strenght of this instant.

To summarise. During training :

- Each moment of satisfaction = Fist Closed
- Fist Closed = Success State
- Success State = information of a state in your Subconscious
-

Do you know that oftently atheletes have charms that they always use before important deadlines. They tell themselves that they won because of this and so that if they re-use it, they will again.

We can explain this belief with Hypnosis. We put so much emotion into this moment, it became a symbol. We all have a very strong image of success. We are conditioned to think that things happens « because of destiny », we want to keep « a good fate ».

However **We are responsible for our victories and defeats.** We are the director/producer of our lives. We give strenght in things outside of us.

This strenght of realisation is **within Us.** You will see that this thought will replace all charms you had before. Trust the fact that you can make yourself a **whole box full of treasure** of success.

You just need to put in place this state during a Trance and to repeat it. It will become a Suggestion. Suggestions can be words, a geometrical form or others, they can be kinesthesic, a move that hold meaning for you, a strenght...

If you want to put a finger up to someone in the street, chances are the meaning will be understood without words. Now you need to build positive suggestions.

Then, outside of training sessions, you need to work on **Mental Imagery.** We already saw this, you just need to put yourself in Auto Hypnosis.

After you have deepened a trance, start to imagine the deadline.

Imagine yourself in the state you want to reach. Take the time to note details of your body, your warming, people managing you. It is essential to **base this work on you.** You are the actor of your action.

Once you well defined the points you chose, go to the context. You are going to imagine your opponents and the course of action you mentaly want.

You can **prepare all scenarios possibles**. Stay focused on Yourself and your emotions. This preparation has to be done the more regularly possible. **At least fifteen minutes a day.**

Preparation for a Professional or Academic deadline

Professional and academic worlds bring loads of tension. I see them as spirit competition. Your body is usually put through a lot. You preparation for deadline has to be a balance body/spirit just like athlete.

It is important that you had a chance to rest before the event you prepare. I noticed that people oftenly come in my practice to prepare an interview or a presentation.

Face to face can be destabilising and, for the more shy of us, heavy. Don't be scared, everything can be prepared and even famous speakers have had fears.

The important is **to put yourself into condition.**

I would advise you to put yourself into trance while in your Comfort Zone. The more you will learn **to relax yourself** the more you will be able to do it everywhere.

The second step is to put yourself into **Active Trance.** Very often we explain that for presentations, you need to repeat many times the same text, arguments, prepare different arguments and counter-arguments.

You are going to **be a one man show.** However you are not going to do it in Conscious Mode. Did you know that Theater Professional are always into trance when they play ?

You are going to do the same thing.

- Choose a Bridge
- Deepen
- Open your eyes keeping the higher state.

You start playing in your head your meeting. In this state you are going to **multiply your perceptions.** You will easily correct yourself and make it normal. Once you start **being satisfied,** you are going to do as the athletes, make a discrete move each time that you succeed.

You can do a simple move like **joining your thumb and index.** In the same way that earlier, you will record physically and emotionally, this state of success and satisfaction. You will make disappear step by step what hinder the most : **the doubt.**

Don't forget that in Auto Hypnosis you multiply your positive suggestibility. You are going to be able to increase your qualities and strengths.

The D-Day

In Sport or professionaly, you are going to do the same. You put yourself into Trance **when you wake up** and go through all you worked and anticipated.

Activate your move, to feel the strenght and trust accumulated. Minutes from the start, repeat your move and breathe simply without thinking of something else than your goal. Your body and spirit will align towards **a better being and real comfort.**

You can do it in all areas of your life once you get the principle. Use constantly your move, the more you do and the best it will become.

Move + Positive Emotions + Mental Image+ Repetitions = Powerful Preparation

19 / Disconnection

You can see that the more you work on Self Hypnosis, the more it **is easy to go back into it.** Now you handle easily your Comfort Zone and suggestions.

Where are you at in your goals results ?

It is important **to keep a central line of work** and to complete with sessions more precise. In this chapter we are going to talk about one of the tools which for me is the most useful in Hypnosis. We will call it **Disconnection.** You are going to learn to disconnect yourself of perceptions of unwanted emotions.

We are a **world of perceptions** and all that we live is filtered by our stories, our emotions... You probably live with some wounds made years ago. They make you suffer because you keep the same point of view on the situation.

That is completely normal. The society taught us to take some distance with emotions. The more we are in emotions that we don't handle and the more it is easy to stir masses.

However thanks to this amazing technique that you master more and more, you are going to **be able to disconnect from this negative flow of perceptions.** To be sure that we talk about the same thing, let me give you an example.

When I say that we live through our perceptions, it means that **our memories are lies to the spirit.**

For example, as a kid you hated « foie gras ».

If questioned at this age, your answer was probably « it is disgusting ». You had **a negative image** of it for some reasons.

One day you tested it again and now you love it.

Your perception of this food is completely different and you start to regret the number of times that you refused it before. If someone ask you what you think of your behavior as a child, you would probably answer that it is too bad you could'nt appreciate it at this point.

Your filter of this very same memory will be completely different. Before liking it, you remembered hating it. Now that you like it, you have some regret to not have ben able to enjoy it sooner. However that moment is still the same.

Your filter changed, your perception too and in consequence your emotions. Everyone is ok to say that the past is in the past and that we can't go back.

It is true in term of actions, but not in term of perceptions. A traumatic act is linked to an interaction with a person. We often keep anger, resentment, sadness and diverse emotions about people. Many are those who struggle to continue their relation, lives, work because they keep a **difficult memory** of an interaction.

This connection can be actual or past, sometimes with people who are now gone.

Links we have, positive or negative, can have **an impact on our actual behaviours,** even events from the past. In this exercice of disconnection, we are going to **cut the grip** of people, and as a consequence, events which today doesn't bring us any good. I want to specify something important. When I say to my clients/patients that we are going to disconnect some holds...some of them panick.

They say that they doesn't want **to cut it all** or that they are scared of forgetting this person. I explain to them that **we change our perceptions** to not be in painful situation anymore.

At no moment you are going to make someone disappear, at most **he/she will have no more interest** for you and naturally your memory which is selective will store it in your archives. Are you ready to free yourself from some emotional weights ?

Very good, to start you are going to choose a situation from your life which hurted you.

Write it down :

____

There was certainly one or some people in this memory who have built in you strong emotions.

Write them down :

____

We are going to work, **one person at the time.** Do not hurry. You can do it during your three daily sessions taking one person by session.

- Take a **Bridge.**
- Deepen.
- Go in your **Comfort Zone.**
- Go through a **door** out of your Comfort Zone.
- You find yourself into a very nice Room.
- **Breathe 5 times** very slowly.
- At the end of the fifth time make the person enter the room.
- Imagine the **face to face.**
- He/she doesn't talk and only listen.
- You are going to express **everything that you have to say,** on him/her, the situation, all you felt, lived...
- Take the time you need and breathe well.
- Once you said it all, you are just going to notive that between him/her and yourself there are **plugs,** maybe hundreds between you two.
- When you want, **you will disconnect all of them at once,** to not have any connection whatsoever.
- If you want it and that you hold a dear affection for this person, you can **decide to connect one** by putting in place a **plug** of love emotion.
- And you let this person disappear from the room.
- Go back to your comfort zone.
- You breathe 5 times and get out of your Trance.

You just unplugged from all the emotions this person had created in you. Take a time to think about him/her and the situation and observe how do you feel ?

Note them here :

____

____

You can even repeat this exercice if you think you left some plugs. There is an important point, when I said that you express all in you. You can do it **in all possible ways,** everything can not be said with words.

You can imagine that you send images, emotions maybe you want to hit... **You don't have limits** it is an expression and you master it.

People within emotions + Plugs + Expressions = Disconnection

20 / Open eyes

You saw different **simple techniques** which allow you to use your trances for different goals. There is an important element I find interesting to underline. You certainly perceived that Hypnosis is a **natural state,** happening frequently.

You understood how to use it in a particular way. This state being natural, it is interesting to take the time to live it open eyes. In our daily life we do not necessarly have the time to isolate ourselves.

We live in a crazy rhythm and you are going to wonder when you can practice. Especially if **you do it three times** a day, sometimes in the day you can't find a quiet place. Hypnosis is really extraordinary in the sense that it doesn't ask **any specific prerequisite.**

As you already worked and experienced for a few weeks the different tools given, you can now do it without any precise « contexte ». For example, you take the bus or the underground to go to work. You can while looking, listening and observing around you, **saturate your senses and enter into a trance.**

Your eyes can stay open. You can realise it while walking.

I got used to do while in meetings. You know these meetings that have no interest but for these two or three colleagues...but are so terribly time consuming.

You keep your eyes open on a fixed point and you can deepen with the countdown. While listening with distance to the events. You work especially **your suggestions**.

That actually comes back to what I was saying about one of the precursor in personal development, Joseph Murphy.

You can use your intention and your positive suggestions many times a day, to replace all your ideas by **constructives thoughts for you.** If you regularly practice Jogging, you are in trance during your tour, use it to focus on **positive things.**

Your subconscious will absorbe all that you propose to him and repetition will allow **deep assimilation.** You are the actor of your Hypnosis, choose simply to use it so that it becomes productive for you.

Conclusion

This book wants to be **as simple as possible and** to present the Auto Hypnosis for you to absorb it without any specific knowledge. This discipline is simple, it is **already open** since your childhood. You just didn't had the right command of suggestions and beliefs available.

Today, you take back a bit of this **control** of natural aspect of yourself. Exercices are childish and only ask **repetition.** If you have doubt on your trance, you have two solutions.

Either your know an Hypnotist who can put in place a small session of Hetero Hypnosis. Or you listen to audios to follow different suggestions that can be made. You will observe that the attitude you constantly need is **TRUST.**

If in your goals trust wasn't there...it is the perfect time to work on it. I didn't want to give you all the jargon of the method. The important is that you can **practice.**

Words are different a school from another and you can see that simple words are enough to understand the essential. Once you have mastered all the basic exercises, you will be able to start **more complete Auto Hypnosis.**

These sessions will be longer and closer to what therapists propose. Trance can **change lives,** some have succeed to stop smoking, find back a healthy weight or keep themselves in good health. You are capable of this **and so much more.**

You start a path that doesn't end but bring more that you can ever imagine.

86

October 2012

Le Chesnay/ France

Who is Christophe Pank ?

I am French and live in Paris. I have worked in hypnosis, NPL, personal development and energetic healing for more than a decade. Everyday, I share my experience and knowledge. To optimise my work, I created HnO (Hype-N-Ose) Hypnose in 2010. As psycho-practitioner, I can help people to learn about themselves, to increase their knowledge.

I am now sharing my ideas in essays, videos and audios. The more you open your mind to different ways of thinking, the more you develop your capacity to become who you really are.

Take the time to watch my english Youtube Channel : hnohypnosis and my website : www.hnohypnosis.com